Preserving Irreplaceable Wildlands

Wild Mountains

A BOOK OF POSTCARDS

SIERRA
CLUB
FOUNDED 1892

Pomegranate

SAN FRANCISCO

Pomegranate Communications, Inc.
Box 808022, Petaluma, California 94975
800-227-1428; www.pomegranate.com

Pomegranate Europe Ltd.
Unit 1, Heathcote Business Centre, Hurlbutt Road
Warwick, Warwickshire CV34 6TD, U.K.
44 1926 430111

ISBN 0-7649-2849-X
Catalog No. SC0304

Pomegranate publishes books of
postcards on a wide range of subjects.
Please contact the publisher for more information.

Cover designed by Lisa Alban
Printed in China

13 12 11 10 09 08 07 06 05 04   10 9 8 7 6 5 4 3 2 1

To facilitate detachment of the postcards from this book, fold each card along its perforation line before tearing.

Tim Fitzharris is the monthly nature photography columnist for *Popular Photography*, the world's largest circulating photo periodical. The author and photographer of more than twenty-five books on wilderness and wildlife—including the award-winning *Sierra Club Guide to 35mm Landscape Photography*—he has received much acclaim for his work. Fitzharris's photographs have appeared on the covers of *Life, Audubon*, and a number of other magazines. He recently published *Nature Photography: How to Take Great Pictures in the Great Outdoors*, a deck of Sierra Club Knowledge Cards™, and his work also appears in four other Sierra Club books of postcards; see the inside back cover for titles and for other publications.

To explore, enjoy, and protect the wild places of the earth;

To practice and promote the responsible use of the earth's ecosystems and resources;

To educate and enlist humanity to protect and restore the quality of the natural and human environment;

And to use all lawful means to carry out these objectives.

Wild Mountains
Rocky Mountain bighorn ram

BOX 808022   PETALUMA   CA 94975

Pomegranate

Photograph © Tim Fitzharris

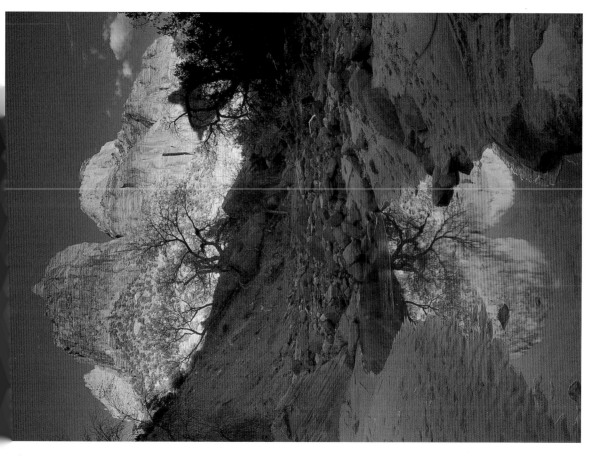

Wild Mountains

Mt. Spry and the East Temple, Pine Creek,
Zion National Park, Utah

BOX 808022   PETALUMA   CA 94975

Pomegranate

SIERRA
CLUB
FOUNDED 1892

Photograph © Tim Fitzharris

Wild Mountains
Porcupine

Pomegranate

BOX 808022   PETALUMA   CA 94975

Wild Mountains
Sierra Nevada Range from Alabama Hills,
California

BOX 808022   PETALUMA   CA 94975

Pomegranate

Wild Mountains
Bull moose

BOX 808022　PETALUMA　CA 94975

Pomegranate

SIERRA
CLUB
FOUNDED 1892

Photograph © Tim Fitzharris

Wild Mountains

Chisos Mountains and century plant

Pomegranate   BOX 80822   PETALUMA   CA 94975

Photograph © Tim Fitzharris

Wild Mountains
Mountain goat

BOX 808022   PETALUMA   CA 94975

Pomegranate

Wild Mountains

Easley Peak, Sawtooth National
Recreation Area, Idaho

BOX 808022   PETALUMA   CA 94975

Pomegranate

Wild Mountains
Mt. Robson, British Columbia

BOX 808022   PETALUMA   CA 94975

Pomegranate

SIERRA CLUB
FOUNDED 1892   Photograph © Tim Fitzharris

Wild Mountains

Blue Ridge Mountains from Doughton Park,
North Carolina

BOX 808022   PETALUMA   CA 94975

Pomegranate

Photograph © Tim Fitzharris

Wild Mountains

Northern saw-whet owl

Pomegranate   BOX 808022   PETALUMA   CA 94975

Photograph © Tim Fitzharris

Wild Mountains

Mount Bellview, near Crested Butte, Colorado

Pomegranate

BOX 808022   PETALUMA   CA 94975

Photograph © Tim Fitzharris

Wild Mountains

Timber wolf pups (captive)

Pomegranate   BOX 808022   PETALUMA   CA 94975

SIERRA CLUB
FOUNDED 1892

Photograph © Tim Fitzharris

Wild Mountains
Mountain lion

BOX 808022   PETALUMA   CA 94975

Pomegranate

Photograph © Tim Fitzharris

Wild Mountains

Brown Mountain, Shenandoah
National Park, Virginia

BOX 808022 PETALUMA CA 94975

Pomegranate

Photograph © Tim Fitzharris

Wild Mountains

Schwabacher Landing,
Grand Teton National Park, Wyoming

BOX 808022   PETALUMA   CA 94975

Pomegranate

Wild Mountains

Wildflowers, Mount Rainier National Park,
Washington

BOX 808022   PETALUMA   CA 94975

Pomegranate

SIERRA
CLUB
FOUNDED 1892

Photograph © Tim Fitzharris

Wild Mountains
Grizzly bear (captive)

BOX 808022   PETALUMA   CA 94975

Pomegranate

Photograph © Tim Fitzharris

Wild Mountains

Lunch Creek Cascades,
Glacier National Park, Montana

Pomegranate   BOX 808022   PETALUMA   CA 94975

Wild Mountains

Gray wolf with pup (captive)

BOX 808022 PETALUMA CA 94975

Pomegranate

SIERRA
CLUB
FOUNDED 1892

Photograph © Tim Fitzharris

Wild Mountains

Elk Mountains in autumn, Colorado

Pomegranate   BOX 808022   PETALUMA   CA 94975

SIERRA CLUB
FOUNDED 1892

Photograph © Tim Fitzharris

Wild Mountains
Bobcat kitten (captive)

BOX 808022   PETALUMA   CA 94975

Pomegranate

Wild Mountains
Gyrfalcon (captive) and alpine penstemon

POMEGRANATE   BOX 808022   PETALUMA   CA 94975

Photograph © Tim Fitzharris

Wild Mountains

Mt. Tom, John Muir Wilderness, California

Pomegranate   BOX 808022   PETALUMA   CA 94975

SIERRA CLUB
FOUNDED 1892

Photograph © Tim Fitzharris

Wild Mountains
Golden-mantled ground squirrel

Pomegranate   BOX 808022   PETALUMA   CA 94975

Wild Mountains
Wapiti elk bugling

BOX 808022 PETALUMA CA 94975

Pomegranate

Photograph © Tim Fitzharris

Wild Mountains

Autumn in Green Mountain National Forest,
Vermont

BOX 808022   PETALUMA   CA 94975

Pomegranate

SIERRA
CLUB
FOUNDED 1892

Photograph © Tim Fitzharris

Wild Mountains

Cinnamon-colored black bear

BOX 808022 PETALUMA CA 94975

Pomegranate

Photograph © Tim Fitzharris

Wild Mountains

Atlantic coast from Cadillac Mountain,
Acadia National Park, Maine

Pomegranate

BOX 808022   PETALUMA   CA 94975

SIERRA CLUB
FOUNDED 1892

Photograph © Tim Fitzharris

Wild Mountains
Yellow-bellied marmots

BOX 808022   PETALUMA   CA 94975

Pomegranate